Artlist Collection

THE DOG

BARK TO SCHOOL HANDBOOK

by The Dogs

As told to Howie Dewin

SCHOLASTIC INC.
New York Toronto London Auckland Sydney
Mexico City New Delhi Hong Kong Buenos Aires

ONE BATTERY BUTTON CELL

IMPORTANT BATTERY INFORMATION

Please retain for future reference.

- Use only AG-13 or L1154 size battery only.
- Battery installation and removal should be performed by an adult.
- Use only batteries recommended in this instruction manual.
- Be careful to install the battery with the correct polarity, as indicated.
- Remove battery when replacing.
- Non-rechargeable batteries are not to be recharged.
- Rechargeable batteries are to be removed from the toy before being charged.
- Rechargeable batteries are only to be charged under adult supervision (if removable).
- Only batteries of the same or equivalent type as recommended are to be used.
- The supply terminals are not to be short-circuited.
- Remove exhausted batteries.
- **CAUTION**: Do not dispose of battery in fire. Battery may explode or leak.

UNE PILE BOUTON

RENSEIGNEMENTS IMPORTANTS AU SUJET DE LA PILE

Conserver pour référence ultérieure.

- N'utiliser qu'une pile AG-13 ou L1154.
- La pile doit être installée et retirée par un adulte.
- Utiliser seulement une pile du type recommandé dans les instructions.
- Insérer la pile en respectant la polarité, tel qu'il est indiqué.
- Retirer la pile pour la remplacer.
- Ne pas recharger une pile non rechargeable.
- Une pile rechargeable doit être retirée du jouet pour être rechargée.
- Une pile rechargeable doit être rechargée sous la supervision d'un adulte (si elle peut être retirée).
- Utiliser seulement une pile du même type que la pile recommandée ou d'un type similaire.
- Ne pas court-circuiter les bornes.
- Retirer la pile lorsqu'elle est épuisée.
- **ATTENTION**: Ne pas jeter la pile au feu. Elle pourrait exploser ou couler.

ISBN 0-439-88060-2

12 11 10 9 8 7 6 5 4 3 2 1   6 7 8 9 10/0

Printed in China
First printing, September 2006
Design by Angela Jun

We Dogs know what it's like to be gearing up for a brand-new school year. More than a few of us have spent time in obedience school and really understand just how overwhelming and ruff it can be!

I mean, come on! Who's your best friend? Huh? Who's your best friend? That's right! We are! So listen to your best friends and follow our ten simple bark-to-school rules.

There's nothing better than being prepared — shiny coat, full belly, no fleas, and a few good chew toys tucked away in the old backpack. We Dogs know how to do it right.

So stick with us and we'll all have a great time and a ter-ruff-ic year!

RULE #1: Know Your Daily Schedule

Nothing puts you in the doghouse faster than being in the wrong place at the right time or the right place at the wrong time . . . or worst of all, the wrong place at the wrong time.

Right place! Right time! That's the recipe for success!

(Along with 3 cups of kibble, 2 cups of table scraps, and 1 cup of gravy . . . sorry, we got a little distracted.)

So let's work through everything you need to make sure you've got a schedule that works for you . . . and a schedule that you can remember, too!

Are you in different classrooms with different teachers during your school day or do you stay in the same classroom for the entire day? Either way, you probably have different subjects you study. For each of those subjects, you have to remember to bring certain books and notebooks.

For example, here's a typical class schedule for a first week at obedience school:

DAY	SUBJECT	REMEMBER	WHERE
Monday	Leash Walking	Leash, collar, treats	Sidewalk
Tuesday	Fetching	Ball, stick, treats	Yard
Wednesday	Off-Limits Training	Bed, slippers, treats	Bedroom
Thursday	Tricks	Frisbee, blindfold, treats	Yard
Friday	Table Manners	Food, drink, treats	Kitchen

Now turn the page and starting figuring out your class schedule!

Make a list of all your subjects, when and where you study them (if it's different each day), and what things you have to remember to bring for each subject.

DAY	TIME	SUBJECT	WHERE	REMEMBER

Now make a list of all the other things you do, such as after-school activities, club meetings, sports teams, and hobbies.

DAY	TIME	EVENT	WHERE	REMEMBER
MON				
TUES				
WED				
THUR				
FRI				
SAT				
SUN				

TIP FROM THE TAIL #1:
Don't overdo it! A good schedule always leaves time to relax and have fun. There's nothing worse than a schedule that doesn't let you roll around in the dirt if the opportunity presents itself!

Now put it all together! Use this calendar grid to create your regular weekly schedule.

	MONDAY	TUESDAY	WEDNESDAY
8 a.m.			
9 a.m.			
10 a.m.			
11 a.m.			
Noon			
1 p.m.			
2 p.m.			
3 p.m.			
4 p.m.			
5 p.m.			
6 p.m.			

	THURSDAY	FRIDAY	SATURDAY	SUNDAY
8 a.m.				
9 a.m.				
10 a.m.				
11 a.m.				
Noon				
1 p.m.				
2 p.m.				
3 p.m.				
4 p.m.				
5 p.m.				
6 p.m.				

TIP FROM THE TAIL #2:
There will be lots of weeks with schedule changes. Things like vet appointments and trips to the kennel always come up. A smart dog keeps a careful list of those things in a safe place where it can always be found. We're not saying you need to bury your list, but it works for us. . . .

The Bark-O-Meter scale: Scheduling!

[sad]
Cry!

[angry]
Growl!

[happy]
Bark!

[excited]
Yip!

[bored]
Yawn!

[tired]
Zzzzz.

[scared]
Whimper!

Using the Bark-O-Meter scale, here's how we feel about . . .

GETTING UP EARLY ______________________

BEING ON TIME ______________________

BEING LATE ______________________

SCHEDULE CHANGES ______________________

REGULAR ROUTINE ______________________

BEING BUSY ______________________

Use some of the stickers in the back pocket of this book to rank how you feel about:

GETTING UP EARLY

SCHEDULE CHANGES

BEING ON TIME

REGULAR ROUTINE

BEING LATE

BEING BUSY

RULE #2: Always Know Where Your Food Is!

Now you have your schedule set. *Congratulations!* That will really help you as a student, but it's also very good for another reason. We Dogs have discovered that the very best part of having a regular schedule is that you always know when you'll be eating food again!

We know you probably aren't quite as good at thinking about food, so we've put together the next few pages to help you. If you work really hard, you can think about food *all the time* — just like us!

What's Your Dream Lunch?

Before you can be really good at thinking about food *all the time,* you have to know yourself. Here are some important questions to think about. We've written some of our answers so you can compare them to yours.

What kind of food do you dream about most?
Any kind you eat.

Do you like a school lunch better than a lunch brought from home?
I like any lunch that's mine.

Do you like your lunch hot or cold?
Yes.

What would your dream lunch be?
A meal that lasted from just after breakfast until just before dinner.

How to Build a Power Lunch

Don't let the best part of the day just pass you by. With a little planning, lunch will be a highlight of your school day!

Shopping List (Or: Dear Mom, Please put these in my lunch!)

1. ______
2. ______
3. ______
4. ______
5. ______

Table Guests (Or: Dear Friend, Please join me for lunch!)

1. ______
2. ______
3. ______
4. ______
5. ______

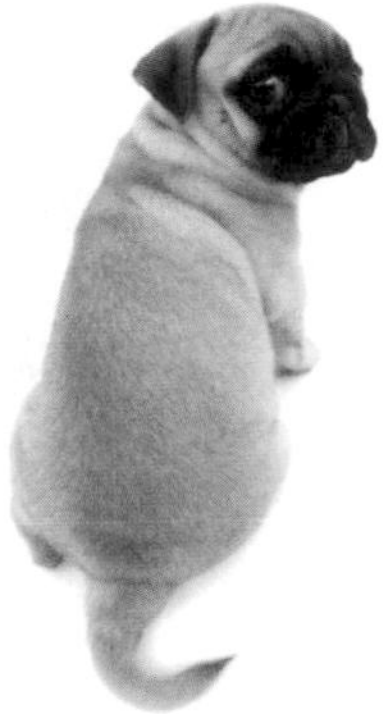

Cafeteria Economics

Not everything equals dollars and cents. We Dogs have known that for a long time. We've been trading bones and kibble for centuries. One of the best ways to create the perfect lunch is through the barter system—*trading*. But you have to know what things are worth! For example:

1 cup kibble = 2 full cans cat food
1 Greenie bone = 4 crunchy bone biscuits

Now figure out what things are worth in your cafeteria. What are kids trading?

1 Twinkie	=	________
1 Chocolate milk	=	________
1/2 PB&J sandwich	=	________
________	=	________
________	=	________
________	=	________

DOGGY DISCLAIMER

We don't eat just because it's the most fun thing in the world. It's also because it's good for us. Food makes us smart and strong and alert. It makes our teeth white and our coats shiny, too.

Signed, *The Dogs*

↑

IT'LL WORK FOR YOU, TOO!

ENERGY FOOD
Brown rice and pasta
Peanut butter
Eggs
Beans
Seeds and nuts

VISION FOOD
Carrots
Sweet potatoes
Peaches
Apricots

BEAUTY FOOD
Citrus fruits
Strawberries
Peppers
Broccoli and spinach
Tomatoes and potatoes

Treats, Snacks, and Rewards

Know your food groups! Treats are entirely different from snacks, which are completely different from rewards. Memorize the following:

Snack — a regularly scheduled nibble
Treats — a surprise from a kind and generous person or dog
Rewards — a payment for good deeds and fine efforts

What are your top choices for each category?

SNACK

____

TREAT

____

REWARD

____

TIP FROM THE TAIL #3:
Know your strengths! You humans have two things we Dogs would really like to have when it comes to getting snacks, treats, and rewards — thumbs and pockets! Boy, oh, boy! If we had thumbs and pockets, we'd be rewarding ourselves *all the time*!

The Bark-O-Meter scale: Food!

[sad]	[angry]	[happy]	[excited]	[bored]	[tired]	[scared]
Cry!	Growl!	Bark!	Yip!	Yawn!	Zzzzz.	Whimper!

Using the Bark-O-Meter scale, here's how we feel about . . .

BREAKFAST

LUNCH FROM HOME

SCHOOL LUNCH

HEALTHY SNACKS

JUNK FOOD SNACKS

MISSING A MEAL

Use some of the stickers in the back pocket of this book to rank how you feel about:

BREAKFAST

HEALTHY SNACKS

LUNCH FROM HOME

JUNK FOOD SNACKS

SCHOOL LUNCH

MISSING A MEAL

RULE #3: Follow the Rules

Rules. Isn't it funny that "rules" sounds a little bit like "growls"? Oh, well, what can you do? If you're a kid — or a dog — you're going to have rules, especially in school. The best thing you can do is figure out how to follow them and still have a good time! (It is possible, if you think about it!)

Here are a few examples. . . .

FOLLOW THE RULE:

Bring the stick back to your owner after you fetch it.

BUT HAVE A GOOD TIME:

Take the long way around the yard on your way!

FOLLOW THE RULE:

Don't bark at the neighbors.

BUT HAVE A GOOD TIME:

Bark at yourself when the neighbors happen to be nearby.

FOLLOW THE RULE:

Don't beg at the table.

BUT HAVE A GOOD TIME:

Beg on the patio, at the couch, or anywhere else people are eating.

Now you try! List some rules you have to follow at school. Then figure out how you can follow them but still have a good time!

FOLLOW THE RULE: ____________________

____

BUT HAVE A GOOD TIME: ____________________

____

FOLLOW THE RULE: ____________________

____

BUT HAVE A GOOD TIME: ____________________

____

TIP FROM THE TAIL #4:
Having a good time with the rules is fun but it can also be tricky. Just make sure you're not doing something else that you know you shouldn't. You might just want to think about whether your "good time" will make the grown-ups in your life frown or smile. (A smile is better.)

Rules Dogs Would Like to Have:

1. All Dogs must eat at least half of every human meal they see.
2. All Dogs are required to consume at least one slipper a week.
3. All Dogs must run wild for at least one hour a day.

Rules You Would Like to Have:

1. ______________________________

2. ______________________________

3. ______________________________

These are rules we Dogs think are GOOD rules:

1. Don't growl at your friends.

2. Don't bark when someone else is barking.

3. Don't bury your homework.

These are rules we Dogs think are BAD rules:

1. Keep food on high shelves.

2. Don't chew on the teacher's desk.

3. Don't shed in the cafeteria.

What are the best and worst rules in your life?

GOOD **rules:**

BAD rules:

Rules you would change if you ran the school:

The Bark-O-Meter scale: Rules!

[sad] Cry!	[angry] Growl!	[happy] Bark!	[excited] Yip!	[bored] Yawn!	[tired] Zzzzz.	[scared] Whimper!

Using the Bark-O-Meter scale, here's how we feel about . . .

NO TALKING

NO PASSING NOTES

NO SNACKS IN CLASS

NO RUNNING IN THE HALL

NO TARDINESS

NO DAYDREAMING

Use some of the stickers in the back pocket of this book to rank how you feel about:

NO TALKING

NO RUNNING IN THE HALL

NO PASSING NOTES

NO TARDINESS

NO SNACKS IN CLASS

NO DAYDREAMING

RULE #4: Be the Best Best Friend Ever!

As experts in best-friend-ness, we want to encourage you to treat every friend like a best friend. Because the truth is, you can never have too many friends — especially with a new school year just starting.

In our humble opinion, *best friends* are:

1. **Loyal**
2. **Trustworthy**
3. **Honest**
4. **Helpful**
5. **Encouraging**

What do you think are the most important qualities in a best friend?

How many people can you name that have the qualities you listed?

TOP TEN WAYS TO BE A *Best Friend*

by The Dogs

10. Put your head in their lap regularly.
9. Don't drool on them while they're eating.
8. Bring them things whether they ask for them or not.
7. Don't have accidents where they're trying to walk.
6. Don't sit in front of the TV when they're trying to watch.
5. Wag your tail every time you see them, even if they just left the room for a minute.
4. Howl quietly.
3. Don't bury their toys.
2. Leave some food for them.
1. Don't yell at them for shedding. They can't help it.

TOP TEN WAYS TO BE A *Best Friend*

by You

10. ______________________________

9. ______________________________

8. ______________________________

7. ______________________________

6. ______________________________

5. ______________________________

4. ______________________________

3. ______________________________

2. ______________________________

1. ______________________________

Buddy! Pal! Sport! What do your friends call you? Here are a few nicknames we Dogs use just for fun. A lot of the time, a nickname is just the opposite of what you'd expect when you look at someone.

Dachshund "Stretch"

Labrador Retriever "Fetch"

German Shepherd "Junior"

Greyhound "Fats"

Beagle "Nose"

Chihuahua "Boss"

Do your friends call you by a nickname? ______________________________

Do you like it? ______________________________

Is there a nickname you'd like better? ______________________________

Do your friends have nicknames?

FRIEND	**NICKNAME**
______________	______________
______________	______________
______________	______________

TIP FROM THE TAIL #5:
Nicknames are only fun if *everyone* thinks they're fun. Before you start calling your friends by new names, make sure they are okay with the name!

The Bark-O-Meter scale: Friends!

[sad]
Cry!

[angry]
Growl!

[happy]
Bark!

[excited]
Yip!

[bored]
Yawn!

[tired]
Zzzzz.

[scared]
Whimper!

Using the Bark-O-Meter scale, here's how we feel about . . .

BEING IN CLASS WITH OUR BEST FRIEND

EATING LUNCH WITH OUR GANG OF FRIENDS

MAKING NEW FRIENDS

HELPING A FRIEND IN NEED

Use some of the stickers in the back pocket of this book to rank how you feel about:

BEING IN CLASS WITH YOUR BEST FRIEND

EATING LUNCH WITH YOUR GANG OF FRIENDS

MAKING NEW FRIENDS

HELPING A FRIEND IN NEED

RULE #5: Communicate!

Communication is the key to success. Of course, we Dogs define success differently from how you do. You probably want to get a good report card. We just want to get a treat. But either way, we both have to know lots of different ways to communicate to reach our goals.

For example, if we're supposed to sit, we might be given a hand signal, a whistle, or one spoken word. There are lots of ways to be told to sit. But the bottom line is this — if we sit, we get a snack.

If you listen hard, look carefully, and speak clearly in school, you'll probably get a really good report card!

Have you figured out this year's buzz words yet?

Just like when you know you're in trouble if your mom uses your whole name, after a while you can get to know your teachers in the same way.

How does your teacher let you know you're about to be in trouble? What does your teacher say to let you know something is a joke?

Think about what words your teacher uses, how your teacher speaks (fast, slow, loud, soft), and the way your teacher moves. You'll find you're getting a lot more information than you even realized!

Listen Up!

What words does your teacher use and how does your teacher speak when . . .

You're very close to getting into trouble: ______________________

It's okay to laugh: ______________________

It's time for silence: ______________________

You've done something impressive: ______________________

Watch Closely!

How does your teacher use body language to let you know . . .

You need to stop talking NOW: ______________________________

You did a great job: ______________________________

The class is waiting for you: ______________________________

You need to try harder: ______________________________

Speak Up!

There's a lot to be said for the way you say things. You can end up at the head of the class or in the doghouse just because of the way you say something. (Not everyone who says SIT gets us to sit.) If you want people (and dogs) to listen to you and respect what you say, you need to think about what you say and how you say it. What would you say in these situations? How would you say it?

You have been caught passing a note to your friend.

____

____

You would like permission to go to the bathroom during a test.

____

____

TIP FROM THE TAIL #6:
Ask questions. One of the most important parts of communicating is getting the information you need. If you don't know something or are confused by something, ask questions until the situation makes sense.

There are other kinds of communication, too. In fact, some communication is completely silent. We Dogs have our ways of passing along coded messages that have to do with certain smells. You humans don't do that kind of thing, but you do pass notes!

Figure out this code and then see if you can write your own message using the code.

D4 y45 n4t kn4w th1t p1ss3ng n4t2s 3n cl1ss 3s 1g13nst th2 r5l2s?!

____

____

____

Your coded message:

____

____

____

(Code: 1:a, 2:e, 3:i, 4:o, 5:u, 6:y)

The Bark-O-Meter scale: Communication!

[sad]
Cry!

[angry]
Growl!

[happy]
Bark!

[excited]
Yip!

[bored]
Yawn!

[tired]
Zzzzz.

[scared]
Whimper!

Using the Bark-O-Meter scale, here's how we feel about . . .

NOT UNDERSTANDING A JOKE

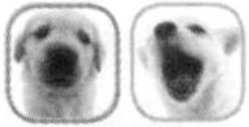

LAUGHING WITH FRIENDS

BEING YELLED AT

NOT BEING ABLE TO HEAR SOMEONE SPEAKING

EXPLAINING SOMETHING CLEARLY

Use some of the stickers in the back pocket of this book to rank how you feel about:

NOT UNDERSTANDING A JOKE

LAUGHING WITH FRIENDS

BEING YELLED AT

NOT BEING ABLE TO HEAR SOMEONE SPEAKING

EXPLAINING SOMFTHING CLEARLY

RULE #6: Find Ways to Solve Problems

We understand how important friends are. After all, we Dogs are pack animals. There's nothing we like more than being with our pack. But that doesn't mean you always agree on how to pull the sled or chase the cat. Being friends is the best thing in the world, but it can be really hard, too.

The important thing to remember is that you can't pull the sled by yourself, so you always need to find a way to solve problems. In fact, solving problems with your friends is something dogs and people have been doing for a very long time!

OLD-FASHIONED DOG WISDOM

1. Bark softly but carry a heavy bone.
2. Walk a mile with another dog's paws.
3. A bone is worth a thousand words.
4. The bark stops here.
5. Loose lips snap sticks.
6. Don't judge a dog by its fur.
7. Beauty is in the eye of the barker.
8. Dogs in glass houses may throw balls.
9. When in Germany, do as the Shepherds.
10. Bark at others as you would have them bark at you.

Can you think of some human sayings that might be helpful when it comes to solving problems with your friends?

1. ______________________________

2. ______________________________

3. ______________________________

Are you good at finding solutions to problems with your friends? Can you find solutions for these situations? Write down your ideas. Then ask your friends how they would solve the problem.

PROBLEM:

There is a group of really popular kids at your school. You and your best friend have not been a part of this group, but have always kind of wanted to be. One day, you get invited to the birthday party of a girl in that group. Then you realize your best friend was not invited. What would you do?

SOLUTION IDEAS:

PROBLEM:

You are at a friend's house with a group of your friends. There are no adults around. One of your friends suggests you all go to the mall together without telling any adults or getting permission. Nobody else seems to think it's a bad idea. At least no one is saying anything. Would you say something?

SOLUTION IDEAS:

PROBLEM:

Your friend is gossiping about someone else in your class. You don't know the other person very well, but you think that person is nice and doesn't deserve to be treated badly. On the other hand, your friend is being really funny and you are having a hard time not laughing. Plus, your friends are all enjoying the gossip, too. What do you do?

SOLUTION IDEAS:

PROBLEM:

This time you're the one being left out. A girl who you've always been nice to is having a party and everyone was invited but you. At least, that's what it seems like. What do you do?

SOLUTION IDEAS:

TIP FROM THE TAIL #7:
Sometimes the best thing you can do to fix a problem is to listen.

The Bark-O-Meter scale: Problem Solving!

[sad]
Cry!

[angry]
Growl!

[happy]
Bark!

[excited]
Yip!

[bored]
Yawn!

[tired]
Zzzzz.

[scared]
Whimper!

Using the Bark-O-Meter scale, here's how we feel about . . .

FIGHTING WITH OUR BEST FRIEND

SHARING OUR BONES AND TOYS

INVITING NEW FRIENDS INTO OUR PACK

LISTENING TO GOSSIP ABOUT OTHERS

HAVING ALL DIFFERENT KINDS OF FRIENDS

FINDING OUT A FRIEND IS IN TROUBLE AND NEEDS HELP

Use some of the stickers in the back pocket of this book to rank how you feel about:

FIGHTING WITH YOUR BEST FRIEND

SHARING YOUR BONES AND TOYS WITH YOUR FRIENDS

INVITING NEW FRIENDS INTO YOUR PACK

LISTENING TO GOSSIP ABOUT OTHERS

HAVING FRIENDS OF ALL DIFFERENT SIZES, SHAPES, COLORS, AND TEXTURES

FINDING OUT A FRIEND IS IN TROUBLE AND NEEDS HELP

RULE #7: Be Well Groomed

Let's face it. Grooming is not just for Poodles. We're not saying you have to get pom-poms shaved onto your elbows or puff-balls put on your ears, but you do have to think about some of the basics — a bath, a shampoo, and a little toothbrushing.

After all, somebody is going to have to sit next to you in school, and you don't want them distracted by a silly thing like flies buzzing around your head!

Here's our basic checklist. How close is it to yours?

1. Soap bath
2. Fur trim
3. Nail trim
4. Teeth polishing

What else do you think is important to keep yourself well groomed?

1. ______________________________

2. ______________________________

3. ______________________________

4. ______________________________

Doggy Dos

Once you get your hair clean, what are you going to do with it? Might we Dogs suggest a few styles you may not have thought of? Find a small picture of yourself. Ask permission to cut your face out of the picture. Then place your face in the middle of the hairdos on these two pages. Which breed suits you best?

Poodle Primp

Sheepdog Sheer

Yorkie Cut

Chihuahua Chop

Bassett Hound Bob

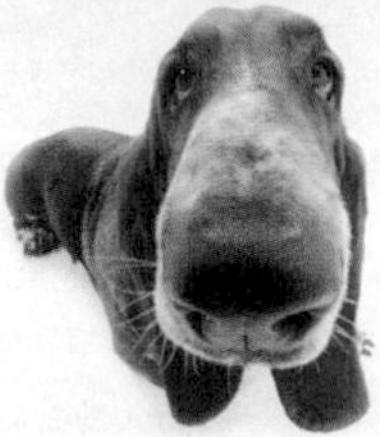

Afghan Do

Collie Coif

Cocker Spaniel Curls

What to wear? There are so many choices. Leather collar or chain? Sweater? Booties? Answer these questions to help figure out how much clothes mean to you. How do your answers compare with your friends' answers?

1. What's most important to you when it comes to clothes?

a) Not thinking about it at all in the morning
b) Wearing what everyone else is wearing
c) Comfort
d) Having the newest style

2. How much do you like to shop?

a) I would rather stick needles in my eyes.
b) Once a year is enough.
c) It's fun with someone else's money.
d) It's my favorite sport.

3. How many favorite stores do you have?

a) None. I've blocked all shopping experiences.
b) Ask my mom. She does all my shopping.
c) Any store that sells sporty clothes
d) I have never been in a store I didn't like.

Mostly A's: Clothes are the last thing on your mind!
Mostly B's: You like to fit in, but you don't like to fuss over your clothes.
Mostly C's: Clothes are fun, but not your favorite thing.
Mostly D's: You're big into style!

These are the fashion trends I like:

1. ____________________
2. ____________________
3. ____________________
4. ____________________
5. ____________________

These are the fashion trends I don't like:

1. ____________________
2. ____________________
3. ____________________
4. ____________________
5. ____________________

TIP FROM THE TAIL #8:
Appearances aren't everything. Some of the smallest dogs are the most ferocious!

The Bark-O-Meter scale: Grooming!

[sad]
Cry!

[angry]
Growl!

[happy]
Bark!

[excited]
Yip!

[bored]
Yawn!

[tired]
Zzzzz.

[scared]
Whimper!

Using the Bark-O-Meter scale, here's how we feel about . . .

A BATH

A NEW OUTFIT

A GOOD FUR CUT

WEARING THE SAME OUTFIT AS OUR FRIEND

A WHOLE DAY OF SHOPPING

FASHION MAGAZINES

Use some of the stickers in the back pocket of this book to rank how you feel about:

A BATH

A NEW OUTFIT

A GOOD FUR CUT

WEARING THE SAME OUTFIT AS YOUR FRIEND

A WHOLE DAY OF SHOPPING

FASHION MAGAZINES

RULE #8: Know What You Like, What You Don't Like, and When You Need a Good Excuse

We all have things we really like and some things we don't. But if your life is like ours, it probably doesn't matter whether you like something or not. You probably still have to do it — or not do it, as the case may be.

(You might be thinking about "math" right now, or maybe "no passing notes." We're thinking about "not eating the steak that's sitting at the edge of the counter.")

So even though you probably won't be allowed to ignore the things you don't like, it's good to keep track of them. That way, you can be sure to have your excuses ready when you need them!

✻ DOG OBEDIENCE SCHOOL SUBJECTS FROM BEST TO WORST

1. Rewards and How to Give Them
2. Naps and How to Take Them
3. Games and How to Play Them
4. Leashes and How to Use Them
5. Cats and How to Respect Them

✻ YOUR SCHOOL SUBJECTS FROM BEST TO WORST

1. ______________________________
2. ______________________________
3. ______________________________
4. ______________________________

Best Dog Excuse for Worst School Subject:

That was the cat? I'm sorry. I thought it was my new squeaky toy.

Your Best Excuse for Worst School Subject:

____

____

What things do you like best and least about the subjects listed on the following pages? Make your lists (from best to worst) and then think of the best possible excuse for that thing you like least!

DOG TEST RESULTS FROM BEST TO WORST

1. Snacks for getting the right answers.
2. Getting the right answers.
3. Accidentally taking a nap in the middle of a test.
4. No snacks for getting the wrong answers.
5. Getting the wrong answers.

YOUR TEST RESULTS FROM BEST TO WORST

1. ______________________________
2. ______________________________
3. ______________________________
4. ______________________________
5. ______________________________

Best Dog Excuse for the Worst Thing About Tests:
I thought this was an "opposites" test. I gave the wrong answers on purpose!

Your Best Excuse for the Worst Things About Tests:

____

____

TIP FROM THE TAIL #9:
No matter what else you do, don't sniff your neighbor's test. Cheating is everybody's least favorite thing!

DOG ASSIGNMENTS FROM BEST TO WORST

1. Dig up things in our yard.
2. Bury things in our yard.
3. Study upholstered furniture.
4. Practice sitting.
5. Take care of a bone like it was our baby.

YOUR ASSIGNMENTS FROM BEST TO WORST

1. ______________________________
2. ______________________________
3. ______________________________
4. ______________________________
5. ______________________________

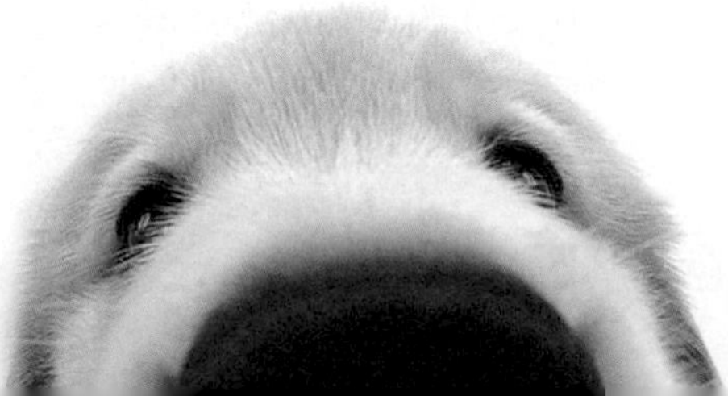

Best Dog Excuse for Worst Assignment:
I ate my homework.

Your Best Excuse for Worst Assignment:

____

____

DOG GYM FROM BEST TO WORST

1. Running.
2. Barking.
3. Fetching.
4. Not having a cool gym collar.
5. Getting picked last for Touch Fetch.

YOUR GYM CLASS FROM BEST TO WORST

1. ______________________________
2. ______________________________
3. ______________________________
4. ______________________________
5. ______________________________

Best Dog Excuse for the Worst Thing About Gym:

I was standing behind the Wolfhound. Nobody could see me.

Your Best Excuse for the Worst Thing About Gym:

____

____

DOG SCHOOL THINGS FROM BEST TO WORST

1. Lunch.
2. Making new friends.
3. Learning new tricks.
4. No barking allowed.
5. Following rules all the time.

YOUR SCHOOL THINGS FROM BEST TO WORST

1. ______________________________
2. ______________________________
3. ______________________________
4. ______________________________
5. ______________________________

Best Dog Excuse for Worst Thing About School:

Rule? Rule!? You said "rule"? I thought you said "drool." I thought you said I had to follow the drool. So I did! And it led me all the way over here!

Your Best Excuse for the Worst Part of School:

____

____

The Bark-O-Meter scale: Bests, Worsts, and Excuses!

[sad]	[angry]	[happy]	[excited]	[bored]	[tired]	[scared]
Cry!	Growl!	Bark!	Yip!	Yawn!	Zzzzz.	Whimper!

Using the Bark-O-Meter scale, here's how we feel about . . .

DOING WHAT YOU'RE SUPPOSED TO DO

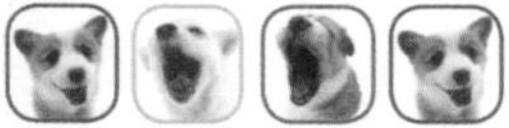

GIVING AN EXCUSE

BEING TOLD AN EXCUSE

LETTING A FRIEND CHOOSE HIS/HER FAVORITE THING

REALIZING YOU LIKE SOMETHING YOU USED TO DISLIKE

DOING JUST WHAT YOU WANT TO DO ALL THE TIME

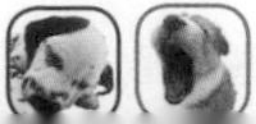

Use some of the stickers in the back pocket of this book to rank how you feel about:

DOING WHAT YOU'RE SUPPOSED TO DO

GIVING AN EXCUSE

BEING TOLD AN EXCUSE

LETTING A FRIEND CHOOSE HIS/HER FAVORITE THING

REALIZING YOU LIKE SOMETHING YOU USED TO DISLIKE

DOING JUST WHAT YOU WANT TO DO ALL THE TIME

RULE # 9: Remember Where You've Been

If you can't depend on your nose to tell you where you've been and what you've done, there are other ways to remember what's happened in your life.

We recommend burying your keepsakes, but we know you humans don't think that's so great . . . so here are a few other ways:

1. Keep a scrapbook.
2. Work on the school newspaper.
3. Join the yearbook committee.

What are the three most important things that have happened so far this year that you would include in a scrapbook or an article?

1. ______________________________
2. ______________________________
3. ______________________________

Whatever you do, keep a journal. Write a little bit every day and you'll be amazed at how interesting it will be a year from now to read what you wrote. Here's your chance to start!

Date:____________________

A Dog Looks Back – The First Days of Obedience School

This is me before I learned some manners.

It's hard to concentrate with so many new friends everywhere!

All of my peeps—I mean, *pups!*

The old ball and chain.

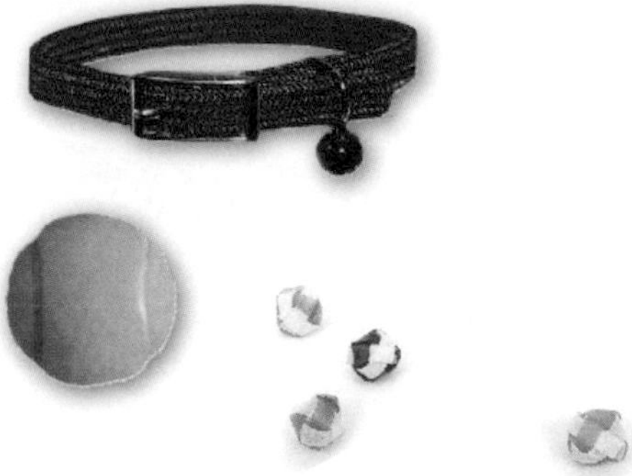

This Year So Far . . .

Use these two pages to collect photographs, words, mementos—whatever helps you remember how this year has felt so far.

The Bark-O-Meter scale: Memories!

[sad]
Cry!

[angry]
Growl!

[happy]
Bark!

[excited]
Yip!

[bored]
Yawn!

[tired]
Zzzzz.

[scared]
Whimper!

Using the Bark-O-Meter scale, here's how we feel about . . .

SHOWING PICTURES TO FRIENDS

READING SOMETHING WE WROTE IN KINDERGARTEN

THINKING ABOUT SUMMER VACATION

REMEMBERING THE FIRST DAY OF SCHOOL

LOOKING AT FAMILY PHOTO ALBUMS

REMEMBERING A FIGHT WITH OUR FRIEND

Use some of the stickers in the back pocket of this book to rank how you feel about:

SHOWING PICTURES TO FRIENDS

READING SOMETHING YOU WROTE IN KINDERGARTEN

THINKING ABOUT SUMMER VACATION

REMEMBERING THE FIRST DAY OF SCHOOL

LOOKING AT FAMILY PHOTO ALBUMS

REMEMBERING A FIGHT WITH YOUR FRIEND

RULE #10: Keep Yourself Busy

School is really important, but it's good to have other things that keep you busy, too. For example, we like to lie on the couch and chew on rawhide. You might have some other ideas.

TOP TEN FAVORITE DOG ACTIVITIES ★

10. Bark.
9. Bark at a friend.
8. Bark for a treat.
7. Run.
6. Run to chase ball.
5. Run to chase stick.
4. Lie on couch.
3. Lie on couch to chew slipper.
2. Lie on couch to chew rawhide.
1. Be with our families.

What are your ten favorite things to do that don't have to do with reading, writing, and arithmetic?

1. ____________________
2. ____________________
3. ____________________
4. ____________________
5. ____________________
6. ____________________
7. ____________________
8. ____________________
9. ____________________
10. ____________________

Have you done any activities that happened at school but didn't have to do with schoolwork? In other words, *extracurricular* activities?

Are there extracurricular activities you would like to do this year?

What clubs, teams, or activities are there at your school? How big a list can you make? How many have you tried? How many do you want to try?

CLUBS

1.
2.
3.

TEAMS

1.
2.
3.

ACTIVITIES

1.
2.
3.

Have you taken years of ballet or judo or art? If you could tell someone five things you've done to let them know more about you, what activities or hobbies would you include?

1. ______________________________

2. ______________________________

3. ______________________________

4. ______________________________

5. ______________________________

Sometimes the answer is in the smallest detail.
The Dachshunds

Looks aren't everything.
The Bulldogs

There's nothing better than a quiet sit on a satin pillow to calm the nerves.
The Pekingese

Stay busy and pay attention and you'll be fine!
The German Shepherds

Make sure you can see the board.
The Afghan Hounds

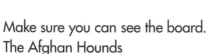

You're never too big for a hug.
The Bernese Mountain Dogs

And now give yourself a pat on the back!

Dear Me,

I think you're the greatest because . . .

ARF-ARF! WOOF-WOOF! We BOW-WOW to you!

MY GOALS

I, ______________________, would like to accomplish the following goals in the coming school year.

1. ______________________
2. ______________________
3. ______________________
4. ______________________
5. ______________________
6. ______________________
7. ______________________
8. ______________________
9. ______________________
10. ______________________

PROGRESS CHART

	OCTOBER	DECEMBER	MARCH	JUNE
1.				
2.				
3.				
4.				
5.				
6.				
7.				
8.				
9.				
10.				

THINGS TO REMEMBER: A new school year is filled with new teachers, friends, routines, locker combinations, clubs and meetings, necessary supplies. . . . You name it, there's something new about it! Here's a place to make a few notes until you get used to the new routine:

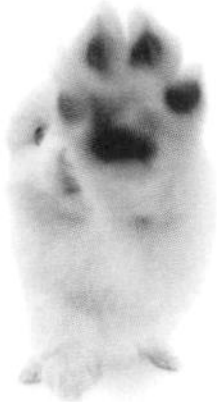

Good Luck!

Have a Grrrrrrreat Year!

The Bark-O-Meter scale: Activities!

[sad]
Cry!

[angry]
Growl!

[happy]
Bark!

[excited]
Yip!

[bored]
Yawn!

[tired]
Zzzzz.

[scared]
Whimper!

Using the Bark-O-Meter scale, here's how we feel about . . .

TEAM SPORTS

ART PROJECTS

CHESS, CHECKERS, AND ONE-ON-ONE GAMES

ACTING, SINGING, DANCING

ANIMALS

TRAVEL AND EXPLORING

THE DOGS' LIST OF THINGS WE HAVEN'T TRIED AND PROBABLY WON'T . . .

1. Knitting
2. Molecular biology
3. Scuba diving
4. Piano
5. Salad

YOUR LIST . . .

1. ______________________________
2. ______________________________
3. ______________________________
4. ______________________________
5. ______________________________

TIP FROM THE TAIL #10:
You don't have to try everything, but it's good to be adventurous. How else do you think Poodles figured out they liked to swim and Terriers figured out they were good at climbing down mole holes?!

YOU CAN DO IT!

You've got a big year ahead with lots of fun and lots of challenges. Let the people around you help you do the very best job you can! Use these pages to gather some encouraging words from your family and friends. Then, if you find yourself having a tough time, you'll know just where to come to get a little encouragement!

Words of Wisdom from *Mom:*

From *Dad:*

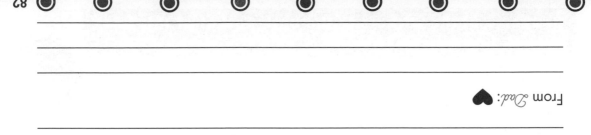

Use some of the stickers in the back pocket of this book to rank how you feel about:

TEAM SPORTS

ART PROJECTS

CHESS, CHECKERS, AND ONE-ON-ONE GAMES

ACTING, SINGING, DANCING

ANIMALS

TRAVEL AND EXPLORING

A Few Words of Doggy Advice

When in doubt, fetch something.
The Labs

We recommend sniffing out the answer. Works every time!
The Beagles

Be who you are — tall, short, round, or thin.
The Corgis

Never underestimate the power of a good haircut.
The Poodles

Most troubles can be outrun.
The Greyhounds

We can spot a hotshot a mile away, and you are on fire!
The Dalmatians

HOORAY FOR YOU!

Encouraging Words from Your Friends:

From *Grandparents:*

From *Aunts, Uncles, and Cousins:*

From *Siblings:*